Watery Worlds

THE OPEN OCEAN

Jinny Johnson

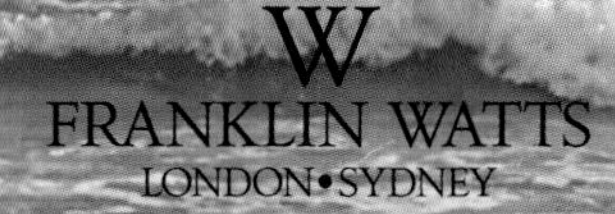

FRANKLIN WATTS
LONDON•SYDNEY

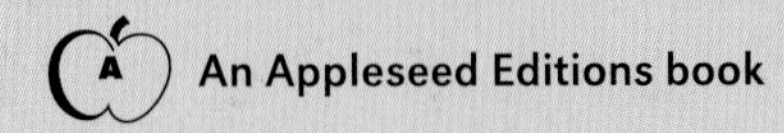

An Appleseed Editions book

First published in 2011 by Franklin Watts
338 Euston Road, London NW1 3BH

Franklin Watts Australia
Hachette Children's Books
Level 17/207 Kent St, Sydney, NSW 2000

Created by Appleseed Editions Ltd,
Well House, Friars Hill, Guestling,
East Sussex TN35 4ET

Designed by Hel James
Edited by Mary-Jane Wilkins
Picture research by Su Alexander
Artwork by Graham Rosewarne

ISBN 978-1-4451-0375-4
Dewey Classification 577.7

A CIP catalogue for this book is available from the British Library.

Picture credits
Title page Wolfe Larry/Shutterstock; Contents page Fedorov Oleksiy/Shutterstock; 4-5 background Wolfe Larry/Shutterstock; 5 Holbox/Shutterstock; 6 OSF/Photolibrary; 7t OSF/Photolibrary, b Peter Arnold Images/Photolibrary; 8-9 background Fedorov Oleksiy/ Shutterstock; 8 Kojiky/Shutterstock; 9t Khoroshunova Olga/Shutterstock, b CBPIX/ Shutterstock; 10-11 background Wolfe Larry/Shutterstock; 10 WaterFrame-Underwater Images/Photolibrary; 11 OSF/Photolibrary; 12-13 background Fedorov Oleksiy/Shutterstock; 12 Christian Wilkinson/Shutterstock; 13t David Thyberg/Shutterstock, b Michael Zysman/ Shutterstock; 14-15 background Fiona Ayerst/Shutterstock; 14 & 15t Animals Animals/ Photolibrary; 15b Fiona Ayerst; 16-17 background Fedorov Oleksiy/Shutterstock; 16 Rostislav Ageev/Shutterstock; 17t Arvydas Kniuksta/Shutterstock, b OSF/Photolibrary; 18-19 background Lakov Kalinin; 18 OSF/Photolibrary; 19t WaterFrame-Underwater Images/Photolibrary, b OSF/Photolibrary; 20 Rich Carey/Shutterstock; 21t J Henning Buchholz/Shutterstock, b Imagebroker.net/Photolibrary; 22-23 background Wolfe Larry/ Shutterstock; 22 Pacific Stock/Photolibrary; 23 & 24 Peter Arnold Images/Photolibrary; 25 OSF/Photolibrary; 26-27 background A Cotton Club/Shutterstock; 26 Schalke Fotografie/ Shutterstock; 27t Andre Nantel/Shutterstock, b Steve Noakes/Shutterstock; 29 Photolibrary; 30-31 Fiona Ayerst
Front cover main image Andre Nantel/Shutterstock, below left to right: CBPIX/Shutterstock, Rich Carey/Shutterstock, David Thyberg/Shutterstock

Printed in Singapore

Franklin Watts is a division of Hachette Children's Books, an Hachette UK company.
www.hachette.co.uk

Contents

Far from land

Sea covers two thirds of our planet and there are huge areas of ocean far away from land. There are not as many animals living here as there are in the sea by coastlines, but some creatures do find food in the open ocean.

Most barnacles cling to rocks in coastal areas, but buoy barnacles live in the open sea. They bob around at the water surface, held up by bubbly **floats** *they make for themselves.*

Amazing!

Only about ten per cent of all sea creatures live in the surface waters of the open ocean.

The female ocean sunfish produces an amazing number of eggs – as many as 300 million at a time.

Guess what?

The ocean sunfish is one of the heaviest of all fish and weighs as much as a tonne – more than a large horse. This strange fish is about three metres long and looks like a large head with a tail attached!

Some of the most powerful hunters in the sea live in these endless waters. Many swim very fast as they travel huge distances to find food or escape from **predators**.

One of the problems for smaller creatures in the open ocean is that there are fewer places to hide than in rocky coastal waters or **coral reefs**. Some fish gather in huge groups – called **schools** – to stay safe, or they hide under driftwood or patches of seaweed. Jellyfish defend themselves by stinging their enemies.

Tiny animals and plants

Some of the most important animals in the ocean are so tiny that we can't see them without a **microscope**. These are plankton, which are creatures that drift in the water. Many different animals, large and small, eat them.

There is both animal plankton and plant plankton in the oceans. Some animal plankton, such as snails and worms, spend only the first part of their lives drifting as plankton. Animal plankton eat each other and they also eat plant plankton. These tiny plants can only live in the surface waters of the oceans. They need the sun's energy to help them grow, just as land plants do.

This animal plankton is shown at many times its actual size.

A young crab floats with animal plankton before growing its adult shell.

WATCH OUT!

The amount of plant plankton in the world's oceans has gone down over the last 100 years. Scientists think this may be because the sea is getting warmer.

Amazing!

Just a teaspoon of sea water can hold up to a million tiny plant plankton.

This plant plankton is called a diatom. You can only see it through a microscope.

Schools of fish

Small fish try to stay safe in the open ocean by keeping together. Fish such as anchovies, sardines and herrings gather in groups called schools.

A school of fish all move together and change direction very quickly. This confuses predators. It's hard for a hunter to pinpoint a particular creature and it may miss its target. A predator may catch and eat some fish in a school, but others escape. The fish on the outside of the group are more likely to be caught than those in the centre.

Larger fish and seabirds prey on small fish such as these anchovies. They swim in huge schools to protect themselves.

Barracuda are fierce hunters. Adult barracuda swim and hunt alone but young fish gather in schools.

Ox-eye scad swim in a tightly packed school. Each fish is about 22 centimetres long.

A large school may contain many thousands of fish.

Amazing!

Guess what?

The fish in a school use sense **organs** along the sides of their bodies as well as their eyes to track each other's movements. As soon as one fish changes direction, others sense this and follow.

Floating hunters

A Portuguese man-of-war might look like a jellyfish, but it's really a group of separate animals. They all live together and have different tasks. These animals are called **polyps**.

Amazing!

The tentacles of a Portuguese man-of-war are usually about ten metres long, but they can grow as long as 50 metres – that's about half the length of a football field.

At the top of the group of animals is a gas-filled float. The float drifts on the surface of the water and acts like a sail. Under the float are lots of polyps shaped like long tentacles. These are covered with little stingers which the man-of-war uses to **paralyse** and kill its **prey**. Other polyps **digest** the food and produce eggs.

A creature called the by-the-wind-sailor is also made up of a number of polyps. It has a float shaped like a sail that bobs along on the water.

Guess what?

The Portuguese man-of-war, with its stinging tentacles, does not sound very tasty. But loggerhead and leatherback sea turtles, as well as some crabs, catch and eat them without being harmed.

The by-the-wind-sailor's float is about 10 centimetres long.

Ocean wanderers

Huge albatrosses and other seabirds soar over the open ocean, searching for food. An albatross sometimes flies 500 kilometres in a day and in windy weather it can glide for hours while hardly moving its wings.

Albatrosses land on the water to grab fish and squid from just below the surface. They also follow ships and feed on food waste which sailors throw overboard. These birds come to land only to **mate**, lay eggs and look after their chicks.

Amazing!

The wandering albatross has the longest wings of any bird. They measure 3.4 metres from tip to tip – that's nearly as long as two adults lying head to toe.

The red-billed tropicbird is a strong flier and a good swimmer.

Tropicbirds and frigate birds also spend most of their life flying over the open sea. Tropicbirds dive down into the water to catch fish and squid, but the frigate bird snatches its food from the surface.

Frigate birds sometimes chase other seabirds and steal their catch.

WATCH OUT!

Many albatrosses and other seabirds are accidentally caught on fishing lines. These long lines have lots of baited hooks and when the birds try to eat the bait they become trapped and drown.

Great white sharks

Amazing!

The great white has an extraordinary sense of smell. It can sniff out a tiny drop of blood in the water fro several kilometres away.

The mighty great white shark is one of the fiercest fish in the sea and it is the biggest hunter. It grows to more than 4.5 metres long and weighs 2,000 kilograms – more than a rhinoceros.

The huge mouth of a great white is lined with jagged teeth, which can be 7.5 centimetres long. The shark uses them to attack and kill its prey.

Great white sharks often swim close to the surface with their large back fin above the water.

It mainly eats seals, sea lions and small whales, but it will snap up anything that comes its way, even animals that are already dead. The great white has a **streamlined** body and powerful tail. These help it cut through the water at up to 24 kilometres an hour as it chases prey.

A great white shark is a top predator and can kill almost anything in the sea.

WATCH OUT!

We are all afraid of sharks, but sharks should be scared of us. Fishermen kill millions of sharks every year. Many are caught just for their fins, which are used to make sharkfin soup.

Giant sharks

The whale shark usually swims slowly, at about one kilometre an hour. It can swim at nearly four kilometres an hour in short bursts.

Not all sharks are fierce hunters. The biggest of all sharks is the whale shark. It grows up to 20 metres long (longer than a bus) and it is also the largest fish. It glides along, **filtering** huge amounts of tiny plankton and small fish from the water.

Another giant is the basking shark, which feeds in the same way. It swims along with its huge mouth open, taking in huge mouthfuls of water and filtering plankton.

Amazing!

A whale shark has the thickest skin of any animal. It is about 10 cm thick – the thickness of a coffee mug.

The whale shark's gaping mouth measures more than 1.5 metres across.

The basking shark can probably filter as much water as an Olympic swimming pool holds in just an hour.

WATCH OUT!

People have hunted basking sharks for many years. They catch them for their meat, the oil in their liver, and their fins, which they use to make sharkfin soup. Basking sharks **breed** and grow slowly and they are becoming **rare**.

The basking shark is the second largest fish in the sea. It can grow to ten metres long.

Long-distance swimmers

Tuna fish are expert hunters and they are built for speed. A tuna has a sleek, streamlined body that narrows near the tail, which is shaped like a half moon. Tuna swim huge distances across the open ocean to find food.

The biggest tuna is the bluefin, which can grow more than four metres long and swim faster than 70 kilometres an hour when chasing prey. The bluefin eats smaller fish, squid and eels and it also filters tiny zooplankton from the water. Other large tuna are the bigeye, yellowfin and skipjack.

Bluefin tuna travel long distances and can swim across the Atlantic Ocean in less than 60 days.

Skipjack tuna often swim in schools and live in warm and tropical parts of all oceans.

The biggest tuna ever caught weighed an amazing 679 kilos – that's more than eight or nine people.

Amazing!

The fast-moving yellowfin tuna can be two metres long and weigh 200 kilos.

WATCH OUT!

Bluefin tuna is rare in the Atlantic and Mediterranean because fishermen have caught too many. The **World Wildlife Fund** asks people not to buy this kind of tuna, so that fishermen will stop catching it.

Manta rays

Guess what?
Smaller fish called remoras often live alongside mantas. They grab scraps of the manta's food and also feed on tiny creatures called parasites that live on the manta's skin.

Manta rays are huge fish with flattened bodies and fins like wings. They live in warm and tropical seas all round the world and they are related to sharks.

Manta rays are the largest of the 500 kinds of ray. The biggest manta ray ever seen measured an amazing nine metres across. Most mantas are about four metres across – still big enough for two tall people to lie across the fish's body.

A manta swims by flapping its large fins and sometimes makes great leaps out of the water.

Mantas feed only on tiny plankton animals and small fish. The fish funnels these into its mouth with the help of the fins on either side of the mouth.

Amazing!

A manta's eggs grow inside her body. She gives birth to one or two live young, which can measure 1.2 metres wide at birth.

The manta ray seems to fly through the water as it flaps its large fins.

Fast swimmers

The speedy blue marlin sometimes leaps above the water surface as it swims.

Sailfish, marlin and swordfish can move very fast when they hunt in the open ocean. They are easy to recognize as they have a very long upper jaw which looks like a sharp spear.

These fish prey on schools of small creatures such as sardines. They swim into a school of fish and slash them with their spearlike jaws. Then they gobble up the fish. These hunters also use their spears to protect themselves against sharks and killer whales.

A swordfish attacks prey with its long, flat, swordlike jaw.

Amazing!

Sailfish are the fastest swimming fish in the sea and can speed through the water at 110 kilometres an hour over short distances.

Guess what?

The sailfish gets its name from the huge fin on its back that looks just like a sail. It can fold this away into a groove on its back when it is swimming fast.

Blue whales

The blue whale usually swims at about eight kilometres per hour, but can speed up to 32 kilometres per hour.

Blue whales are the biggest animals in the sea and probably the largest animals that have ever lived on Earth. A whale is a **mammal**, not a fish, and it has fins instead of legs. It spends all its life in water, but has to come to the surface to breathe air.

A blue whale can grow to 30 metres long – at least twice as long as a bus. This gigantic creature leads a quiet life and feeds mainly on plankton, particularly shrimplike **krill**, which it filters from the water. It sometimes eats as many as 40 million a day! Blue whales usually live alone, except for mothers caring for their young.

Amazing!

A blue whale's tongue weighs as much as an elephant!

Guess what?

A baby blue whale is seven metres long at birth – longer than three people lying head to toe. The baby feeds on its mother's milk for up to eight months and drinks nearly 400 litres a day – that's about four bathfuls!

A blue whale swims with her calf.

Dolphins

Dolphins are small whales. They spend some time near coasts, but they also travel in groups called pods across the open ocean. There can be several hundred dolphins in a pod. Dolphins are expert swimmers and often leap out of the water as they travel.

Like whales, dolphins are mammals and have to come to the water surface to breathe.

WATCH OUT!

More than 300,000 dolphins, whales and porpoises die every year when they are caught in fishing lines or nets and drowned. Many are also hit by boats and ships.

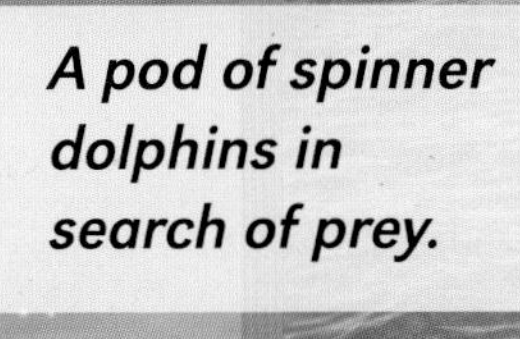

A pod of spinner dolphins in search of prey.

All dolphins are predators and catch fish and squid with their sharp teeth. Some dolphins work together when hunting and **herd** fish into tight balls, which they then gobble up. They keep in touch with each other by making lots of different clicking, squeaking and whistling sounds.

Amazing!

Dolphins look after sick or injured animals in their family or pod and help them to the surface so they can breathe.

World oceans: Arctic

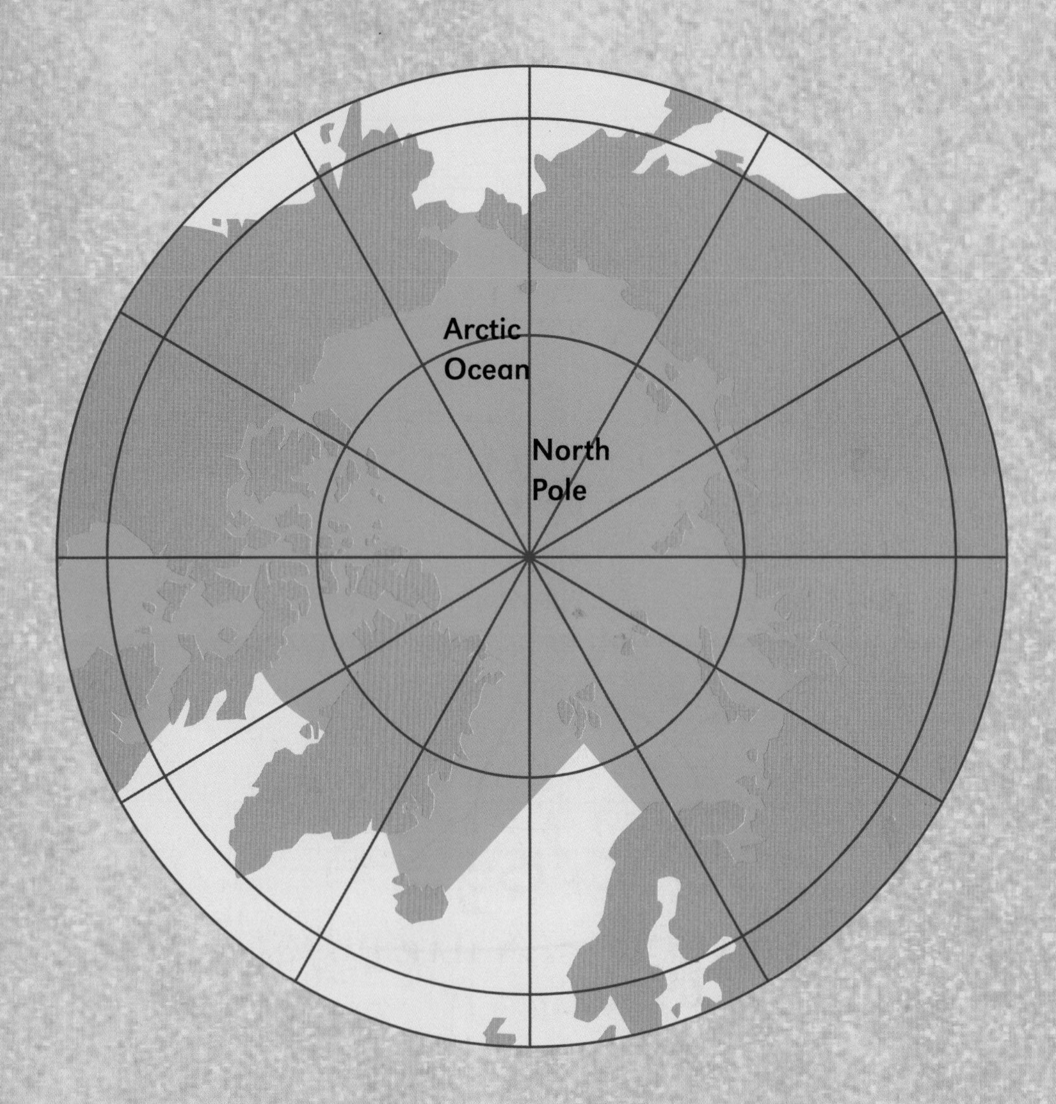

The Arctic Ocean is the smallest of the world's oceans. Most of it lies north of the Arctic Circle near northern Asia, Europe and North America. The water is so cold that the middle part of the ocean is covered with thick ice all year round. This area of ice is nearly twice as big in winter. The Barents Sea, Chukchi Sea, Hudson Bay and Baffin Bay are all part of the Arctic Ocean.

Arctic Ocean facts

The Arctic Ocean covers an area of about 14,056 square kilometres. That's almost one and a half times the size of the United States.

The first expedition known to reach the North Pole at the centre of the Arctic was led by the American explorer Robert E. Peary in 1909.

The Arctic ice cap is growing smaller because of global warming. Scientists are worried that the melting ice could cause sea levels to rise all round the world.

The deepest point of the Arctic Ocean is the Fram Basin, which is 4,665 metres deep.

Many rivers flow into the Arctic, including the Ob, the Yenisey and the Lena from Siberia and the Mackenzie from Canada.

Explorer Robert Peary at his base after his expedition to the North Pole in 1909.

Watery words

breed
To mate and produce young.

coral reef
An ocean area where lots of tiny coral animals live.

digest
To break down food so that it can be used by the body.

filter
To strain from the water.

float
The gas-filled part of a creature such as the buoy barnacle that floats on the water surface and supports the animal.

herd
To drive a group of creatures together.

krill
Small shrimplike animals.

mammal
A warm-blooded animal that feeds its babies with milk from its own body. Land mammals have four legs but sea-living mammals, such as whales and seals, have flippers instead.

mate
Male and female animals pair up, or mate, to produce young. An animal's partner is its mate.

microscope
An instrument which you look through and makes tiny objects appear larger.

organ
A part of the body that performs a particular task.

paralyse
To make another animal unable to move.

polyp
A small animal with a soft body.

predator
An animal that hunts and kills other animals to eat.

prey
An animal that is hunted and eaten by another animal.

rare
Something that is not often seen or found.

school (of fish)
Group of fish that swim together.

streamline
To make a neat shape that moves easily through water.

World Wildlife Fund
An organization that works to protect animals and the natural world.

zooplankton
Tiny animals that float in the water. Many larger animals feed on zooplankton.

Index